Come Worship

A CHRISTMAS INVITATION

by Russell Mauldin and Sue C. Smith

Lillenas PUBLISHING COMPANY

KANSAS CITY, MO 64141

Contents

Come and Worship! 4
    Angels, from the Realms of Glory
    Angels We Have Heard on High
    O Come, All Ye Faithful

The Invitation 16

Come, Thou Long-expected Jesus 29

You're Divine 39
    Away in a Manger
    You're Divine

We Settle 53

Joy, Joy! 70

The Birthday of a King *with* O Holy Night 81

Celebrate the Child *with* Go, Tell It on the Mountain 90

The Power of His Name. 105

Worship Christ, the Newborn King 117
    O Come, All Ye Faithful
    Thou Didst Leave Thy Throne
    Joy to the World
    Joy, Joy!

Finale 131
    The Invitation
    O Come, All Ye Faithful
    Angels, from the Realms of Glory

Come and Worship!

Angels, from the Realms of Glory
Angels We Have Heard on High
O Come, All Ye Faithful

Arranged by Russell Mauldin

*"Angels, from the Realms of Glory"

Come and wor-ship. Come and wor-ship.

Wor - ship Christ, the

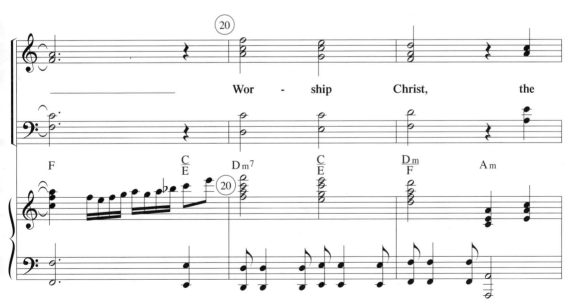

6

new - born King.

G sus   G   C

26

C

26

$\frac{B\flat}{C}$ $\frac{Am}{C}$ $\frac{Gm}{C}$ $\frac{F}{C}$ C^2

CD: 3

*"Angels We Have Heard on High"

30   Unison   mf

Unison   mf   Come to Beth - le -

$\frac{B\flat}{D}$ $\frac{Am}{D}$ $\frac{Gm}{D}$ Dm $\frac{C^2}{E}$ $\frac{B\flat}{C}$ 30   F Am^7

mf

8

10

*"O Come, All Ye Faithful"

12

CD: 7

14

The Invitation

Words and Music by
STEVEN CURTIS CHAPMAN
Arranged by Russell Mauldin

*NARRATOR: Dear Heavenly Father, we invite You to be with us as we celebrate the miraculous birth of Your Son, Jesus Christ. And thank You for inviting us to be with You in these moments. More than ever, we realize the importance of taking time to know You and love You more dearly. Come and meet with us face to face and reveal to us a glimpse of Your glory.

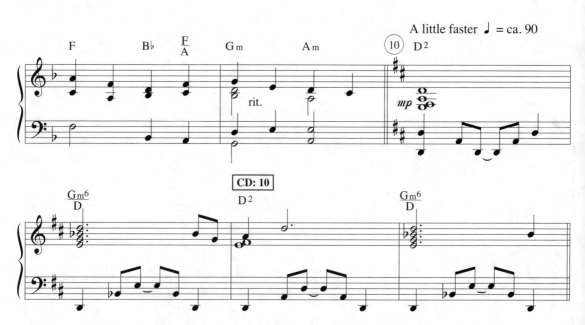

© 1999 Sparrow Songs/Peach Hill Songs (BMI)/Songs On the Forefront/Geoff Moore Songs (SESAC).
All rights administered by EMI Christian Music Publishing. Used by permission.

PLEASE NOTE: Copying of this product is NOT covered by CCLI licenses. For CCLI information call 1-800-234-2446.

18

22

24

Come, Thou Long-expected Jesus

CHARLES WESLEY

RUSSELL MAULDIN
Arranged by Russell Mauldin

ANNA: I was only married for seven years. After my husband died, the temple was the only
place I felt comfortable. God invited me there, and I answered His invitation. In fact, I never
left the temple, which probably led some to believe that I was a bit strange or even crazy.
(music begins) I worshiped Him there night and day– fasting and praying. I was waiting for
the Messiah, the Promised One. I wasn't about to leave the temple and take the chance that
He would arrive without me being there.

30

Hope of all the earth Thou art–

Dear De - sire of ev - 'ry na - tion,

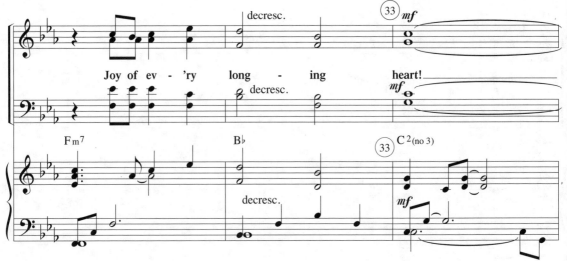

Joy of ev - 'ry long - ing heart!

CD: 17

36

Let   us find our   rest

in   Thee.

rit.

rit.

You're Divine

Solo and Ladies

SUE SMITH

RUSSELL MAULDIN
Arranged by Russell Mauldin

MARY: I thought I knew what my future would be like– marriage, children, a home– a life like so many women before me. But an angel changed my life forever when he told me that I had found favor with God and that I was to give birth to His Son. In my fear and amazement I asked, "How is this possible since I am a virgin?" The angel told me the Holy Spirit would visit me and that God's power would overshadow me. Those words were a calling, an invitation to serve God in a way I could never have imagined. The words moved my soul, and I answered God's call saying, "I am the Lord's servant. May it happen just as you have said."

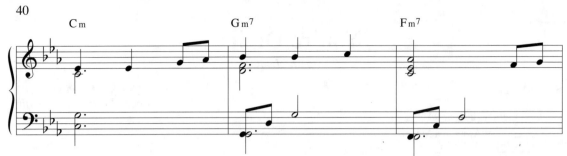

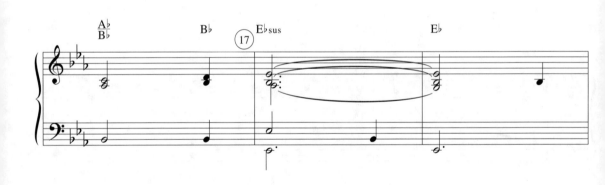

CD: 21 A little faster ♩ = ca. 98

42

44

50

We Settle

SUE SMITH

RUSSELL MAULDIN
Arranged by Russell Mauldin

INNKEEPER: I'm sometimes viewed as the villain in this story. I'm the hard-nosed innkeeper.
The guy with no room in his inn for a fragile mother just on the verge of giving birth. But what
should I have done that night? Should I have thrown out my best paying customers to give her
and that peasant husband of hers a place to sleep? Put yourself in my sandals for a moment.
(music begins)

PLEASE NOTE: Copying of this product is NOT covered by CCLI licenses. For CCLI information call 1-800-234-2446.

56

mir - a - cles God has in mind to do. O yes we

O yes we

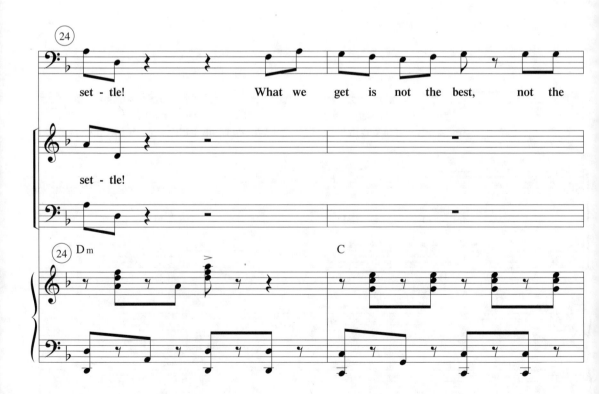

set - tle! What we get is not the best, not the

set - tle!

won - ders that He planned for me and you;

In - stead of

B♭   A7   Dm   D

(28)

And

Divisi

all He wants to give us, we end up with so lit - tle,

Divisi

(28) Gm7   C7   FM7   B♭M7

CD: 29

we miss out on so much more_____ be - cause we

So much more be - cause we

set - tle!   Now if you

set - tle!

(43) was a might-y sold-ier, but De - li - lah caused him grief, So he

Gm7   C/E   F   B♭/D

lost a whole lot more than just his hair. And when Eve

Gm/E   C#°7   Dm   D7

(47) took that bite of fruit she must have tho't it tast - ed sweet, But

Gm7   C/E   F   B♭/D

CD: 30

was it worth the cost we've had to bear?

Gm/E   E7   A

62

63

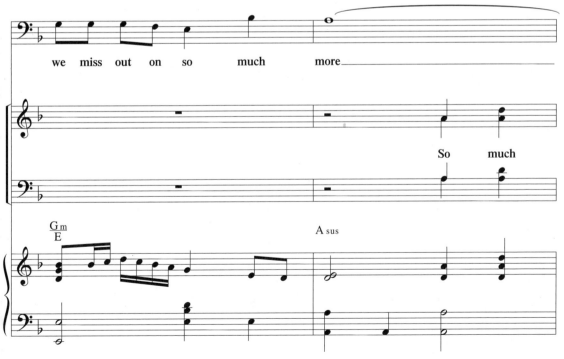

CD: 31

be - cause we set - tle!   It's a

more be - cause we set - tle!

rit.

A   A/G   F+   A⁷/E   D m

(67) Freely ♩ = ca. 90

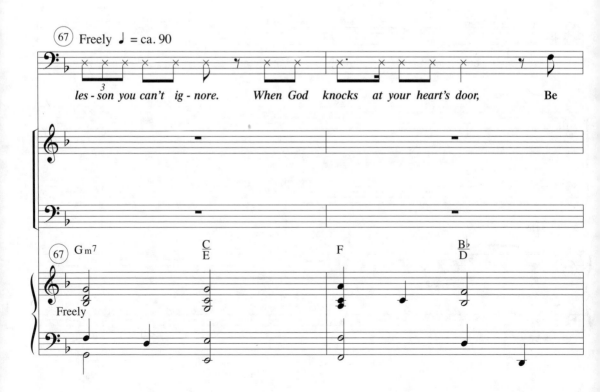

les - son you can't ig - nore.   When God   knocks   at your heart's door,   Be

G m⁷   C/E   F   B♭/D

Freely

66

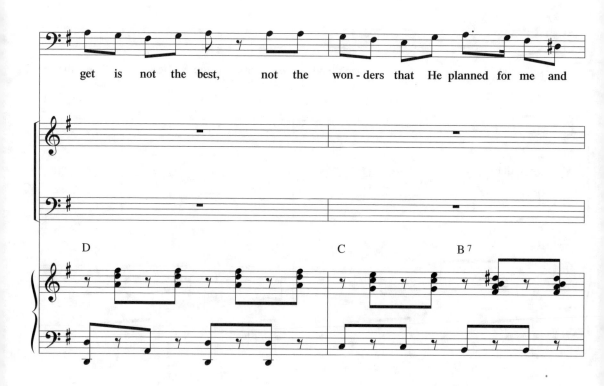

68

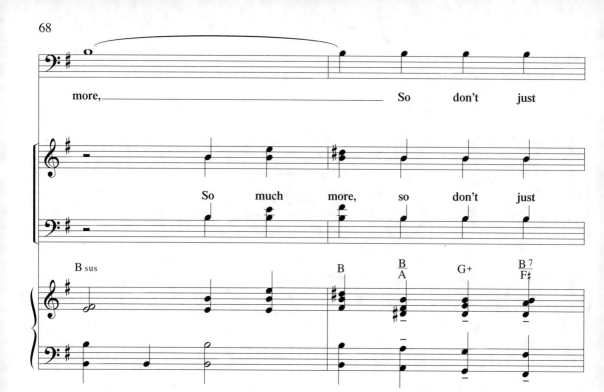

set - tle! *Know the full - ness of His love!* Don't just

set - tle! Don't just

set - tle!_____ *Don't set - tle!*

set - tle!_____ *Don't set - tle!*

set - tle!_____ *Don't set - tle!*

Joy, Joy!

Words and Music by
DAVID PHELPS, MATT HUESMANN
and **WENDY WILLS**
Arranged by Russell Mauldin

SHEPHERD: I know the hills around Bethlehem like the back of my hand, and I've rescued
  sheep in every situation imaginable. I've been in the midst of storms no normal man would
  brave. I've fought off wild animals with no thought for my own life. I've climbed to peaks
  and crawled in muck all for the protection of my sheep. Yes, I consider myself to be very
  brave, at least in situations that I'm accustomed to. But that night *(music begins)* when the
  angels visited us, I was frightened like never before. If they hadn't assured us that there was
  no reason to be afraid, I probably would have fainted dead away. But I remained wide
  awake and heard the incredible thing the angels were there to proclaim.

set. An - gels fold - ed their wings_____ at the

throne wor - ship - ing, as God whis - pered, "I love You, my

Son." Je - sus took off His crown, and

lay - ing it down said, "Fa - ther,_ Thy will be done."

74

Ah,_____

Unison Then God called to Ga - briel with

gladness and tears, "Play the trum-pet, the horns and the

strings." Tell the shep-herds, the wise men, and

78

80

The Birthday of a King

with
O Holy Night

Words and Music by
WILLIAM HAROLD NEIDLINGER
Arranged by Russell Mauldin

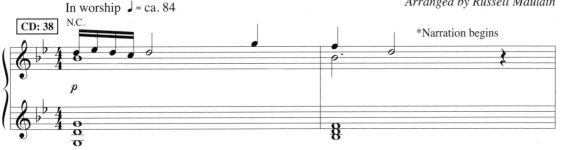

*NARRATOR: I was just part of the crowd of taxpayers in Bethlehem. I didn't know a king was sleeping in a pile of hay meant for donkeys and camels. I was not the only one who didn't receive notification of His arrival. Less than ten miles away at the temple in Jerusalem, the religious leaders received no special announcement. The political officials certainly got no formal briefing. No, only some common, lowly shepherds were on the list of "People to Notify" of His royal birth.

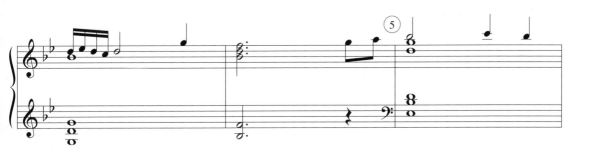

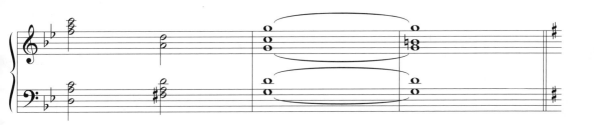

82

CD: 39

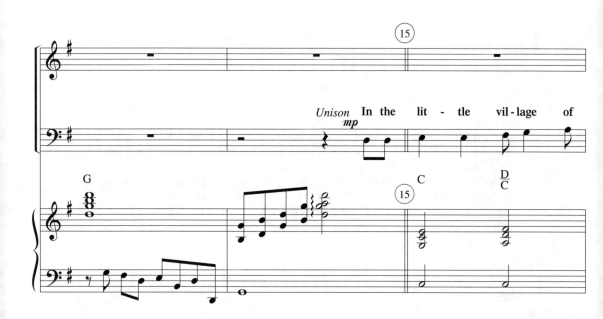

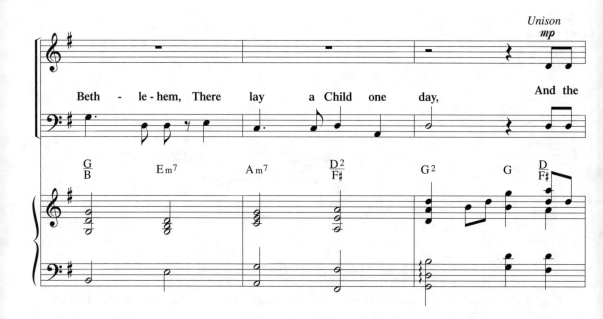

Celebrate the Child

with

Go, Tell It on the Mountain

Words and Music by
MICHAEL CARD
Arranged by Russell Mauldin

Lynn E.

SHEPHERD: Responding to the invitation from the angels, we went into the village. There we found Him just as the angels said. We fell to our knees before Him in awe. *(music begins)* My heart was pounding, my mind racing. I thought, "Is this really the Messiah?" In my heart, I knew it was true. When we finally left that place, we couldn't stop talking about everything we had heard and seen.

CD: 47

CD: 49

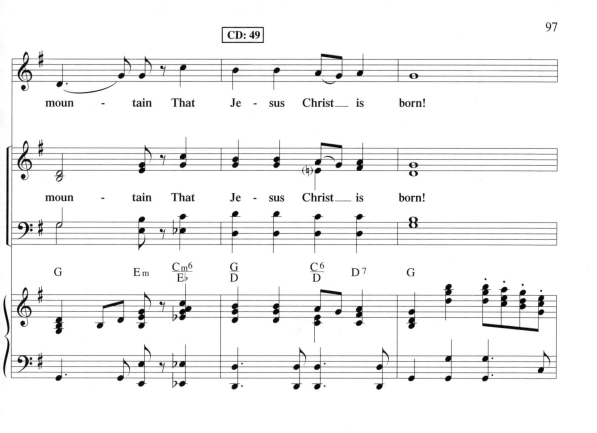

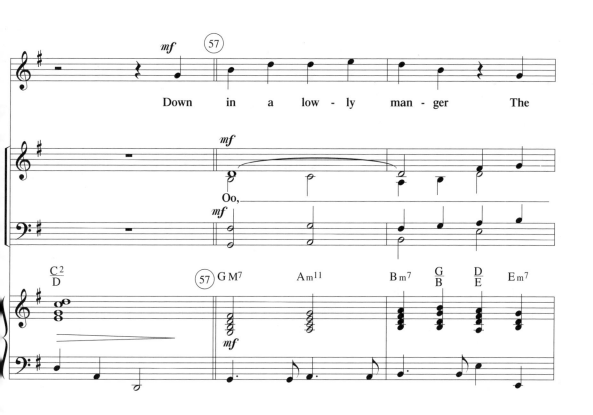

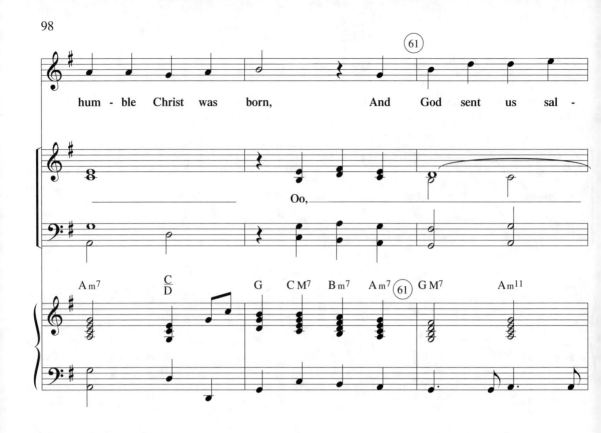

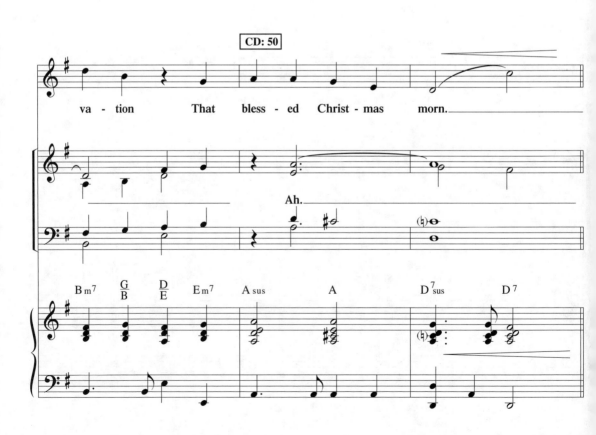

Go,_____ tell it on the moun - tain.

Go, tell it on the moun - tain,

G

We need to

O - ver the hills and ev - 'ry - where;_____

D7   C/D   D7   G   G/B   C   D

100

102

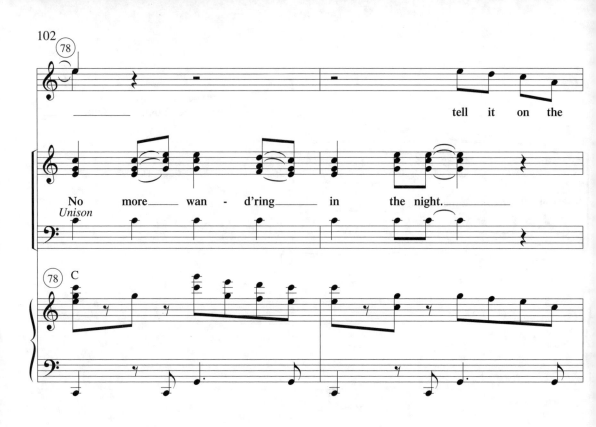

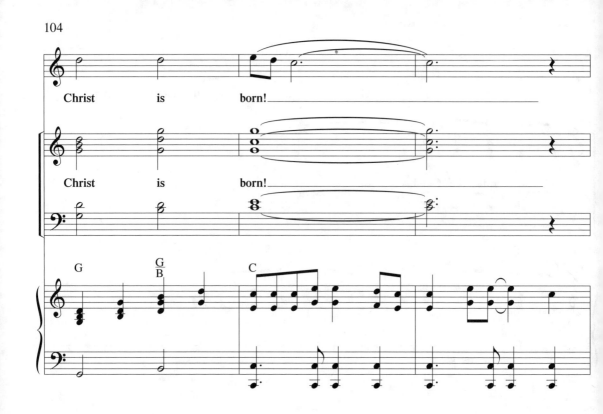

Christ is born!

Cel - e - brate the Child who___ is the Light!

Cel - e - brate the Child who___ is the Light!

The Power of His Name

SUE SMITH

RUSSELL MAULDIN
Arranged by Russell Mauldin

cra - dled Him so gen - tly with whis - pered words of

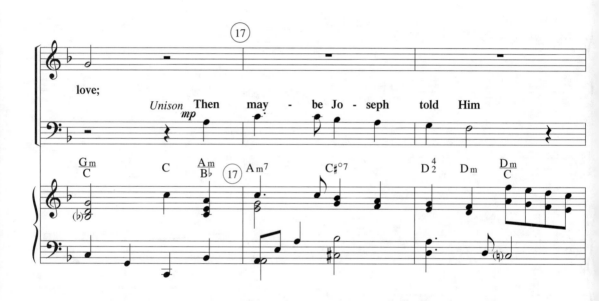

love;

Unison **Then may - be Jo - seph told Him**

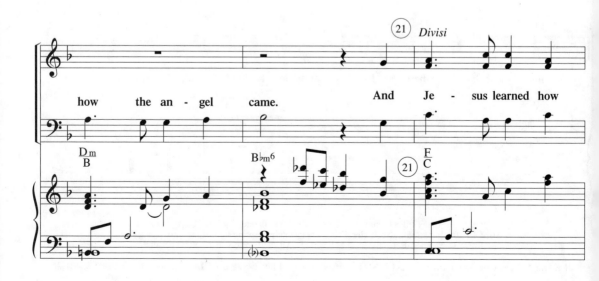

how the an - gel came. And Je - sus learned how

beau - ti - ful   to   sing;   There's   mer - cy   and   sal -

va - tion   on - ly   heav - en   can   ex - plain   in the

glo - ry,   and the pow - er of   His   name.

CD: 56

Worship Christ, the Newborn King

O Come, All Ye Faithful
Thou Didst Leave Thy Throne
Joy to the World
Joy, Joy!

Arranged by Russell Mauldin

WISE MAN: We were educated men, comfortable with combining what we observed
with what we read in the ancient writings. We made a well-informed decision to
follow the star. We knew that if this was the star we had studied, it would lead to
a Child who was the Chosen One, the Messiah.

We were so focused on the fulfillment of prophetic writings, it took us a while
to realize that something was happening in our hearts. *(music begins)* Hours before
we arrived at that simple stable, we started to feel the awesome power of what we
were about to encounter. The star that had invited us out of our homeland led us to
Him, and in His presence, all of our great wisdom seemed so insignificant. Our
wealth was meaningless, our gifts inadequate. But we presented our gifts and
ourselves to Him– knowing we were kneeling before the Son of the living God.

Reverently ♩ = ca. 92

CD: 58 *"O Come, All Ye Faithful"

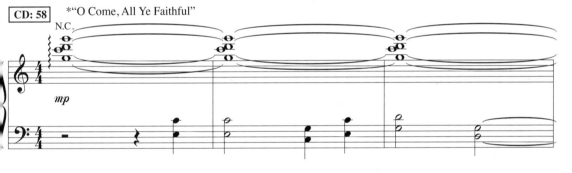

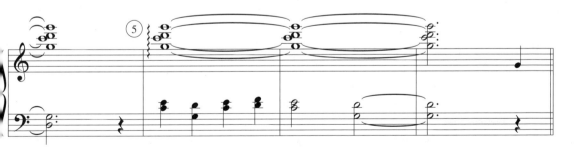

118

CD: 59

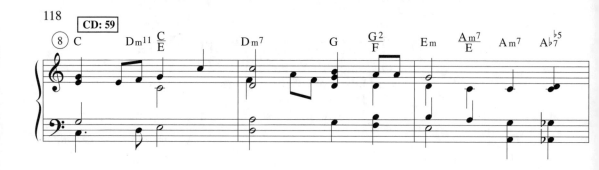

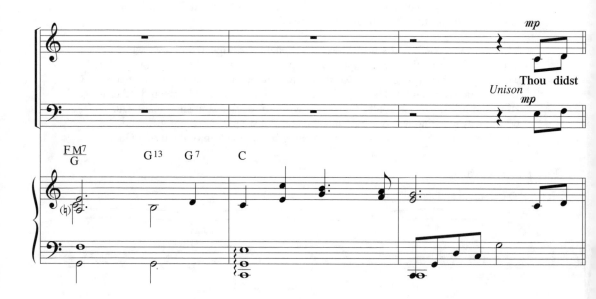

(14) *"Thou Didst Leave Thy Throne"

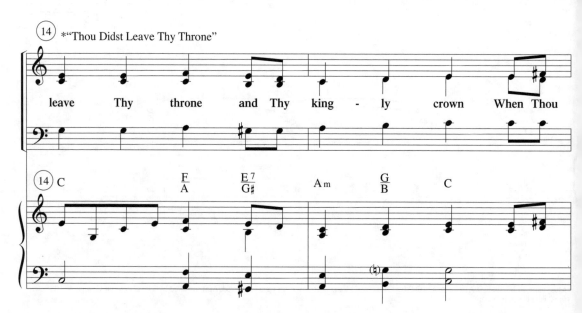

leave Thy throne and Thy king - ly crown When Thou

cam - est to earth for me;_____ But in

E m7   A m7   G sus   G   G/B

Beth - le - hem's home there was found no room For Thy
Divisi

C   D/C   G2/B   G/B   C6   A/C#

ho - ly na - tiv - i - ty._____ O

G/D   D7 sus   D7   D6   G7 sus   G7

CD: 60

120

122

CD: 64

Finale

The Invitation
O Come, All Ye Faithful
Angels, from the Realms of Glory

Arranged by Russell Mauldin

ANNA: The prophecy was fulfilled.

WISE MAN: The King of kings became a helpless baby.

SHEPHERD: A manger became a throne.

INNKEEPER: A stable became a cathedral of worship.

MARY: A baby became the Savior of the world.

NARRATOR: *(music begins)* Heavenly Father, like the people we have met tonight, we rely on our comfort zones, our viewpoints, and ourselves far too much. Because of this, our lives are filled with fear instead of calm, turmoil instead of peace. But You invite us to experience something new. When we say yes to Your invitation, we have access to the strength, power and hope that can only be found in Jesus Christ. You invite us to "Come and behold His glory, the glory of the one and only Son, who came from the Father, full of grace and truth." We accept Your invitation. We have come to worship You.

With emotion ♩ = ca. 96

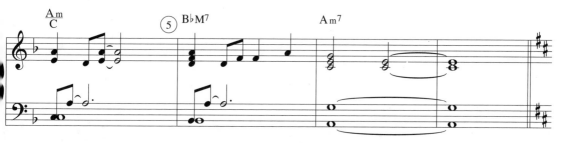

132

So now   will you

134

136

CD: 69

accel.

*"O Come, All Ye Faithful"

Faster ♩ = ca. 108

Yea, Lord, we greet Thee, born this hap - py

morn - ing. Je - sus, to Thee be all

137

140

Come & Worship

Come & Worship

A Christmas Invitation